CONTENTS

KU-512-060

Foreword	5
The Background to the '45	7
The Work of Wade	13
A Prince is Born	16
Prelude to the '45	18
The Rising Begins	19
The Standard is Raised	21
The March South	24
The Battle of Prestonpans	26
The March Continues	29
The Retreat from Derby	32
The Battle of Falkirk	37
The Retreat Continues	40
The Battle of Culloden	41
The Aftermath of Defeat	48
The Prince on the Run	50
Flora Macdonald	52
Return to Exile	55
The Final Years	56
Changes in the Highlands	58
The Legend	59
Places to Visit	62
Index	63

The momentous events of the fourteen months between Prince Charles Edward Stuart's landing in Scotland in July 1745 and his departure in September of the following year entered Gaelic lore as Bliadhna A' Phrionnsa, *The Year of The Prince.*

THE YEAR
OF THE PRINCE

Bliadhna A' Phrionnsa

*The Story of the Jacobite Rising
of 1745–6*

by GAVIN D SMITH

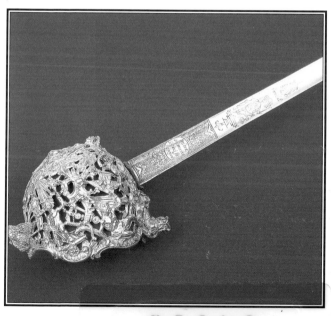

First published in 1995 by
Ross Literary Services Ltd.,
52 Maldon Road,
London, W3 6SZ.

Editor: Jill A. Laidlaw
Picture researcher: Jill A. Laidlaw
Map illustrator: Simon Borrough
Designer: Simon Borrough

J941·1072
914325

Printed in the European Community
by Scotprint Ltd., Musselburgh
The Year of the Prince
ISBN 1 899736 00 X

9 8 7 6 5 4 3 2 1

*Title page: Prince Charles Edward Stuart's basket-hilted sword. According
tradition, it was taken from the Prince's baggage wagon by the Duke of
Cumberland.*

FOREWORD

The Jacobite rising of 1745–6, and the central role of Charles Edward Stuart — Bonnie Prince Charlie — constitute the most dramatic and romantic episode in Scottish history, as well as the most serious threat to the rule of formal law in Britain during the eighteenth century.

This is ultimately a story of tragedy, defeat and retribution, which changed the Highland way of life forever. It is also a story which throws up many instances of remarkable courage and loyalty, played out against a backdrop of incomparable beauty. Little wonder it has become the stuff of legend.

The lasting legacy of Jacobitism is to be found in poems, novels and songs, often of haunting beauty, and it is found too, of course, in battlefields, castles, cairns, museums and visitor centres throughout the Highlands and Islands.

Prince Charles Edward Stuart
as a boy.
By Antonio David, 1732.

In addition to such high-profile testimonies to the Jacobite adventures of 1745 and the previous half century, any number of less well-known reminders still exist.

For example, the room in Perth's Salutation Hotel in which Charles stayed for eight days in September 1745 is still in regular use, and in the churchyard of Finsthwaite near Windermere in Cumbria a white marble cross marks the grave of Clementina Johannes Sobieski Douglas, 'The Finsthwaite Princess'. According to legend, she was the illegitimate daughter of Charles and Clementina Walkinshaw, who was hidden away with a local family.

What follows is an attempt to tell the Jacobite story in factual terms, and also to give some sense of the breadth of the legend beyond the facts, as well as guiding the reader towards those tangible monuments to Jacobitism that still exist in Scotland today (see page 62).

The Background to the '45

It is a common misconception to see the events of 1745–6 and the various Jacobite attempts that preceeded them as some kind of Anglo-Scottish conflict. In fact, this is far from the truth, as the Jacobite cause was by no means universally popular in Scotland, particularly in the Lowlands, and there were many English, Welsh and Irish Jacobite supporters. Jacobitism had as much, if not more, to do with religion than with nationality.

King James VII of Scotland, deposed in the 'Glorious Revolution' of 1688–9.

The story of Bonnie Prince Charlie and the '45 rising has its origins in the overthrow of the reputedly despotic Catholic monarch James VII of Scotland and II of England in the 'Glorious Revolution' of 1688–9. The term 'Jacobite' is derived from the Latin Jacobus — James — and was first used to describe supporters of the deposed King James II, whose aim was the restoration of the Stuart monarchy.

John Graham of Claverhouse — known as Bonnie Dundee.

James' place on the British throne was taken by his daughter Mary and her Dutch Protestant husband, William of Orange, who reigned as joint monarchs from April 1689. The overthrow of James was the signal for a Jacobite rising in Scotland and England, which culminated in victory for the Jacobite forces under John Graham of Claverhouse — known as Bonnie Dundee — at the Battle of Killiecrankie in 1689. Dundee subsequently died of wounds inflicted during the battle, however, and without his leadership the rising petered out.

The Pass of Killiecrankie is owned by the National Trust for Scotland, and the wooded glen thirty miles north of Perth features the famous 'Soldier's Leap', an eighteen-foot-wide gap across the River Garry, which was reputedly jumped by a Williamite soldier, Donald MacBean, as he escaped from Jacobite pursuers. The actual battle was fought about one mile north of the Pass.

Anne — daughter of the deposed and exiled James II — succeeded to the throne on the death of William in 1702, becoming the last Stuart monarch of England and Scotland. The Stuart dynasty had ruled Scotland since 1371 and England since 1603.

After William's death, caused when his horse tripped over a molehill and threw him, Jacobite supporters took to toasting 'The gentleman in the velvet jacket'. One popular Jacobite version of the loyal toast was 'Here's to the King, sir, Ye ken who I mean, Sir'. Glasses were often passed over a vessel of water during this toast to signify allegiance to the Stuarts in exile and later featured engravings of the Jacobite white rose. Sadly for the Stuarts, only a small percentage of those willing to undertake such domestic heroics were prepared to take up arms for the cause they verbally espoused.

During the next half century there were a number of attempts to restore a Stuart monarch to the British throne, most notably in 1715, when the Jacobites rose against the newly crowned King George I, who spoke no English and was known in Scotland as 'The Wee German Lairdie'. This unsuccessful rising culminated in the indecisive Battle of Sheriffmuir, where the Jacobites were led by the Earl of Mar.

> *There's some say that we wan,*
> *And some say that they wan,*
> *And some say that nane wan at a' man,*
> *But, one thing, I'm sure,*
> *That at Sheriff-muir,*
> *A battle there was which I saw, man...*
>
> **Anonymous Scottish ballad**

By this time the focus of Jacobite aspirations against the German house of Hanover was the son of James II — known to history as the Old Pretender — and half-brother to Queen Anne. The term 'pretender' comes from the French word for 'claimant', rather than implying that his claim to the throne was in any way a pretence. Like his father before him, James the Old Pretender was a principled Catholic, and this was destined to limit his support, as was the Jacobite cause's reliance on foreign aid if restoration was to be a practical possibility. The Catholic kingdom of France in particular was vital in this respect, but its participation was almost certain to alienate many potential English supporters, for whom France was always the ultimate enemy.

Four years later another Jacobite attempt (this time with Spanish aid) came to nothing, principally because the Spanish fleet was badly damaged by storms and forced to return to port. As we shall see, this was not the last outbreak of 'Hanoverian weather' to hamper the Jacobites.

A Stuart family tree engraved during the time of Queen Anne.

THE WORK OF WADE

The abortive rising of the '15 left the British government in no doubt that the Jacobite threat was serious, particularly in view of the cause's potential support from Catholic countries in Europe, and they began to introduce measures designed to minimise the impact of any subsequent Jacobite attempts.

A number of barracks were built, including Ruthven, near Kingussie, and in 1725 Major General George Wade was appointed Commander in Chief of Scotland. He supervised the erection of forts at Fort Augustus and at Inverness in the east. Along with the existing base at Fort William to the west, these formed what was known as 'The Chain', stretching along the line of the present Caledonian Canal.

Ruthven Barracks, off the A9 near Kingussie in Inverness-shire, was built in 1719, and was designed to hold a company of soldiers in two blocks. It was the rendezvous point for defeated Jacobite soldiers after Culloden, who subsequently blew it up so that it could not be used by government troops. The ruined barracks are now

in the care of Historic Scotland, and were featured in the 1994 film about the '45, Chasing The Deer. *For the purposes of the film, Ruthven was restored to its state in 1745 by the use of computer imaging techniques.*

The various forts and barracks were linked by Wade with the Lowlands by two hundred and fifty miles of road and forty bridges between 1725 and 1737. Companies of Highlanders loyal to the Crown were established, and these formed the nucleus of what was to become the first Highland regiment of the British army, the Black Watch.

Fort George as it was in 1744 before the Hanoverian government rebuilt it after the '45.

This map details some of General Wade's new roads between Stirling and Inverness.

A PRINCE IS BORN

A year after the 1719 Jacobite attempt, the birth in Rome of Charles Edward Stuart, son of James The Old Pretender and his Polish wife Clementina Sobieski (right), led to a change of focus in Jacobite aspirations by the time of the next and most significant Jacobite rising in 1745.

'The Young Pretender', as Charles became known, undoubtedly possessed many qualities that fitted him to the immense task his destiny provided for him. The courage that was to gain him the respect of so many Highlanders during the 1745–6 campaign was in evidence at an early age. At the battles of Prestonpans and Falkirk only the clan chiefs' assertion that they would return home with their followers unless the Prince was more prudent, prevented him from personally leading his army into battle.

When he was thirteen Charles was present at the seige of Gaeta in Italy, and insisted on visiting the most dangerous positions. As a result of that experience, he determined to seek military glory when he grew up. Accordingly, he proceeded to make himself physically very fit with a regime of walking and riding, and his figure was naturally athletic. In the words of one contemporary, "He seemed made for war".

He possessed all the spirit and decisiveness of his mother, and little of his father's more hesitant character, and clearly he had considerable charisma. It was surely not just loyalty to the cause that meant nobody claimed the vast reward offered by the government for his capture during his time in Britain.

Charles was indeed a bonnie prince, though the sobriquet 'Bonnie Prince Charlie' was never used in his lifetime, but was bestowed on him retrospectively as the legend of the '45 grew. An eye witness account of Charles prior to the Battle of Prestonpans described him as '...a tall slender young Man, about five Feet ten Inches high, of a ruddy Complexion, high nosed, large rolling brown Eyes, long visaged, red-haired, but at that Time wore a pale Periwig. He was in Highland Habit...'

Prince Charles Edward Stuart (right),
with his younger brother Henry (1725–1807).

If Charles was physically well equipped for the daunting task of trying to rescue the throne of Britain for the Stuarts, he was less well off in terms of practical military knowledge, never having studied the art of warfare. Indeed, his studies in general were haphazard, and he was brought up in the somewhat artificial and very insular world of the Jacobite court in exile. This court had been expelled from France and settled in Rome under the protection of Pope Clement XI, one of the few foreign leaders to recognise Charles as king.

PRELUDE TO THE '45

In 1739 Britain again went to war with Spain, and three years later with France. Jacobite hopes began to rise when the French planned a major invasion of Britain to be staged early in 1744.

According to the plan, three thousand French troops were to be landed in the Highlands, where they would join forces with those clans loyal to the Jacobite cause, while a second army, four times this strength, with Prince Charles among its number, was to be landed on the south coast of England, within easy marching distance of London.

In late February the fleet carrying the larger force was ready to sail from Dunkirk when a gale wrecked many of the ships and the French decided to abandon the venture. Once again, the weather had sided with the Hanoverians.

The Prince's fleet is ravaged by storms.

THE RISING BEGINS

Despite this major setback, the frustrated Prince determined to press ahead with his attempt on the British throne, believing, from his somewhat isolated position in France, that he could count on the support of most of the Highland clans once he set foot on Scottish soil. Having been brought up to believe in the British crown as his birthright, Charles was inclined to wait no longer, despite the lack of serious French aid.

In Britain, even the most loyal Jacobites thought the project to be ill-conceived, and begged him to reconsider, but having borrowed money and pawned jewellery to finance the trip, the Prince sailed from Belle-Ile with two ships, the Du Teillay, on which he travelled, and the 64-gun vessel The Elizabeth, carrying a total of some seven hundred men and a quantity of arms.

The Jacobites' ill-luck was to continue, however, and The Elizabeth was intercepted by a British 'man-of-war' off the Lizard Peninsula in Cornwall. The ship was so badly damaged that she had to return to France, taking the seven hundred men and accompanying arms with her.

Despite the loss of The Elizabeth, Charles pressed on, and on 23rd July he and seven supporters landed on the Hebridean island of Eriskay from the Du Teillay. For Charles this was his first sighting of Scotland, the most emotionally significant part of the kingdom he had been brought up to believe was his by right.

Two days later the Du Teillay sailed into Loch nan Uamh on the coast of Arisaig, and at Borradale landed its modest cargo of arms, money and men; an Englishman, three Irishmen, an Ulsterman and only two Scots! These followers were to go down in history as 'The Seven Men of Moidart'.

Today a tangible reminder of those seven men survives in a row of beech trees which stands in a meadow close to the village of Kinlochmoidart. The seven trees were planted in the nineteenth century to commemorate Charles' initial supporters, though one has subsequently been destroyed and the others damaged during storms in 1988. Seven new beeches have recently been planted to guarantee the continuity of this memorial.

The island of Eriskay where Charles trod on Scottish soil for the first time.

THE STANDARD IS RAISED

Once on the mainland, Charles and his band proceeded to Glenfinnan at the head of Loch Sheil, a dozen miles from Fort William, certain that the clansmen of the Highlands would rally to the cause. In reality many of the most pro-Jacobite chiefs greeted the news of his actual arrival with little support and something close to dismay.

The raising of the standard at Glenfinnan.

Nonetheless, 1,300 clansmen rallied immediately to the cause, and on 19th August the Duke of Atholl raised the Stuart standard at Glenfinnan and read a document proclaiming James 'The Old Pretender' as king, and Charles "Sole regent of our kingdom". By this time, the British government had offered a reward of £30,000 (equivalent to more than £1 million today) to anyone who captured the Prince. Charles responded by offering £30 for George II!

Charles himself addressed the assembled Highlanders, but was only later to realise that his fine speech in English was understood by comparatively few of those present, whose native tongue was Gaelic. To the Highlanders, he was Tearlach Mac Sheumais, Charles, son of James, and despite any language difficulty, the patently sincere and imposing figure of the Prince was enough to inspire his troops. So began eight of the most dramatic months in Scottish history.

The Glenfinnan Monument is situated ten miles from Fort William, and is in the care of the National Trust for Scotland. It was erected in 1815 by Alexander MacDonald of Glenaladale, successor to the Glenaladale with whom Charles stayed the night before the raising of the standard, and who accompanied Charles in his months as a fugitive after Culloden. The figure which tops the sixty-five foot tower is not intended to represent Charles, as is often thought, but is a symbolic Highlander, and was added in 1834. Across the Fort William-Mallaig road is a visitor centre, where one may listen to recordings about the raising of the standard in a variety of languages, whilst studying the monument itself. The Gaelic version is particularly atmospheric.

The white rose was chosen in August 1745 as the Jacobite campaign badge, and its representation in ribbon form, worn on the bonnet, was known as the 'white cockade'. The rose bush which provided the inspiration for the choice still flowers at Fassfern, some six miles east of Glenfinnan.

Some of the most important clan chiefs did not 'come out' to join Charles, most notably MacDonald of Sleat, MacDonald of Clanranald, and MacLeod of Dunvegan. Had all the clans that could reasonably have been expected to flock to the Stuart standard actually done so, Charles should have been able to put an army of some 30,000 men into the field.

The most significant recruit to the cause was Donald Cameron the Younger of Lochiel, acting chief of the Camerons, known as 'The Gentle Lochiel', who had many misgivings about the venture yet was to prove one of Charles' most faithful adherents. The Glengarry, Keppoch and Glencoe MacDonalds also pledged their support, and with them and the Camerons 'in', others soon followed.

The West Highland Museum in Fort William contains a fascinating collection of Jacobite memorabilia, including an anamorphic 'secret' portrait of Prince Charles, which looks like a child's colourful scrawl until viewed on a polished metal cylinder, when it reveals a good likeness of the Prince. This portrait was used to toast Charles at a time when possession of a more orthodox painting would have been highly dangerous.

THE MARCH SOUTH

The assembled Jacobite army proceeded to march south and occupy Perth, evading General Sir John Cope, Commander-in-Chief of the government forces in Scotland, and his troops who were marching north to intercept the Jacobite army. From Perth, Charles and his men made a break for the Lowlands and the Scottish capital of Edinburgh, which they occupied on 17th September. So far, progress was most encouraging.

At Perth, Charles acquired his two Lieutenant-Generals, the Duke of Perth and Lord George Murray, youngest brother of the Hanoverian Duke of Atholl, who were to provide the expedition with badly needed military experience. With the exception of MacDonald of Keppoch, who had served in the French army, none of the clan chiefs who initially 'came out' possessed any formal military training.

Murray had been born in 1694, and held a commission in the British army until 1715, when he joined the Jacobites. His eldest brother William, Marquis of Tullibardine, forfeited the title of Duke of Atholl as a result of his role in the rising of 1719, but to the Prince's supporters during the '45 he was the rightful Duke of Atholl, rather than his Hanoverian younger brother. Tullibardine played a central role in the raising of the standard at Glenfinnan. Lord George Murray was also 'out' in 1719, after which he spent six years in exile before being pardoned and returning to a settled family life in Perthshire.

Murray's support for Prince Charles during the '45 came more from a sense of duty than any burning desire for adventure or military glory, though he was to prove the principal architect of two Jacobite victories, and displayed the soundest of judgement on all occasions during the campaign.

Murray was a blunt man with a manner that was frequently overbearing, characteristics hardly calculated to endear him to a sensitive soul like the Prince, who had spent most of his life surrounded by fawning supporters at the Stuart court in exile.

James Drummond, Duke of Perth, had learnt the rudiments of military engineering in France, and despite poor physical health he was a modest and easy-going man, who acted as an excellent foil to Murray.

Blair Castle, the ancestral home of the Dukes of Atholl, lies thirty-five miles north of Perth, and possesses some fascinating Jacobite memorabilia. On the eve of the Battle of Killiecrankie (see page 8) Bonnie Dundee slept at Blair, and it was there that he was to die from his wounds after the battle. Prince Charles stayed in the castle both on the march towards London and again during the retreat north. Lord George Murray laid siege to his Hanoverian-garrisoned home in March 1746. This unsuccessful siege was the last to be laid against any castle in Britain.

At Edinburgh the Jacobites took the city with considerable ease, though the castle held out against them in what was to be its last defence in a long and turbulent history. The Jacobite army arrived at Edinburgh on 16th September and occupied the city until 31st October. A contemporary newspaper report noted that "The Highlanders behave civilly and pay cheerfully for what they get".

THE BATTLE OF PRESTONPANS

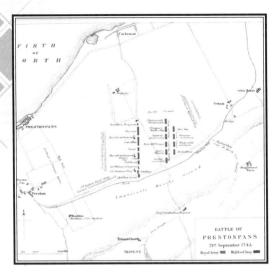

A plan of the Battle of Prestonpans.

A Victorian impression of the Battle of Prestonpans.

Meanwhile, Cope and his forces had sailed to Dunbar, and on 21st September they met the Jacobite army near Prestonpans, close to the Lothian coast a few miles east of Edinburgh. The encounter between two and a half thousand Highlanders and a similar number of government troops was to provide a rude awakening for the crown forces, who were routed in less than ten minutes. This facile victory in the Jacobite army's first encounter was the deciding factor in Charles' plan to march south to take London.

Today the site is marked by a modest cairn, located on the area of the battlefield which remains open country. The battle took place near Bankton House, between the modern AI and A198 roads, and is now in the shadow of Cockenzie power station.

Before setting off for the border, Charles held court at the Palace of Holyrood in Edinburgh, not only entertaining in a regal manner but organising his troops into clan regiments and assimilating new recruits. Most importantly, they included many of the MacDonalds, the Macphersons and the Stewarts of Appin, as well as sufficient Atholl men from Perthshire to form a brigade. Having carefully calculated which way the wind blew, the waverer Lord Lovat also ordered his clan Fraser to take the Prince's side.

How did the Prince's Highland army, some five thousand men far from home and without stores, manage to feed itself and its horses? In his diary, the Edinburgh lawyer-politician Sir John Clerk, a loyal Hanoverian, noted that he had been required to provide 6,000 stones of hay and 76 bolls of oats from his country estate. Men were also billeted on large houses and farms. Clerk's main complaint was about the amount of entertaining he was compelled to do, feeding sixteen or more of the Jacobite chiefs at a sitting. Other leading citizens had to do the same, more or less willingly.

Holyrood Palace

The Grass Market, Edinburgh.

On 31st October Charles and his army left Edinburgh, aware that the bulk of the regular British army would soon return from service in France, and that it would be sensible to try to reach London before their arrival. At the time of Charles' landing less than 4,000 regular troops were in Britain. From the point of view of morale, the victory at Prestonpans was very significant for those loyal to the government, who began to see the threat to London and the established order as very real.

Though George II was far from universally popular, the threat of social and economic chaos by a rebellion for people who were, by and large, enjoying a fair degree of prosperity, was not attractive. Perhaps most importantly, the old fear of 'papacy' was very strong, despite the fact that Charles was less adamantly Catholic than his father.

These fears were prevalent in Lowland Scotland as well as England, and go a long way towards explaining why the Prince did not accrue the level of support he had anticipated as he crossed the border and marched south.

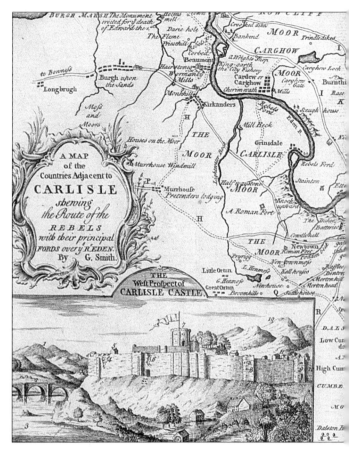

A map of the Jacobite route through Carlisle, engraved after the rebellion.

On 12th November the Jacobites took Carlisle, with Charles marching at the head of the army as it continued through Kendal, Lancaster and Preston, before reaching Manchester on 30th November. As one contemporary observer noted, "He never din'd nor threw off his cloaths at night, eat much at Supper, used to throw himself upon a bed at Eleven

o'clock, and was up by four in the morning. As he had a prodigious strong constitution, he bore fatigue surprisingly well".

Very few of the fifteen hundred or more men the Jacobites had expected to join up on the march south actually materialised, though in Manchester some two hundred were recruited. This 'Manchester Regiment' consisted largely of unemployed men, who admitted that they would have joined whichever army arrived in the city first!

Whilst the Prince was musing on the niceties of whether to enter London on horseback or on foot, his generals and clan chiefs were becoming more pessimistic about the possible success of the venture, in view of the paucity of English recruits to their force. Already retreat was being mooted, but Lord George Murray and the chiefs agreed to go at least as far as Derby before reviewing the position so that nobody could accuse them of not giving Charles as much support as was realistically possible.

31

THE RETREAT FROM DERBY

The Jacobite army arrived at Derby, 127 miles from London, on
4th December, but by this time George II's son the Duke of
Cumberland, with a force of some ten and a half thousand
men, was at Lichfield, whilst Wade and his forces were
marching south from Wetherby in Yorkshire. A third army was
being assembled on Finchley Common to defend London,
where there was real panic and fear at the prospect of the
arrival of a marauding Highland army. In total the government
forces ranged against the five thousand-strong Jacobite army
numbered in excess of thirty thousand troops. It was in this
seemingly impossible position that Lord George urged retreat
to Scotland, supported by virtually all the Jacobite officers.

Another factor that made such a course of action seem
attractive was the rumour that the Duke of Perth's brother Lord
John Drummond had landed in Scotland with a sizeable
French force.

Charles did not appreciate the feeling of the meeting at

An engraving by William Hogarth of volunteers about to depart for Finchley Common to join the army massing to defend London from the Jacobites.

which retreat was discussed, in the long-demolished Exeter House. As Lord Elcho put it, "He fell into a passion and gave most of the Gentlemen that had Spoke very Abusive Language, and said that they had a mind to betray him".

For the rest of his life Charles retained the belief that London could have been taken and the entire enterprise successful if he had not been forced to retreat from Derby.

Retreat he did, however. The 6th December went down in Jacobite circles as 'Black Friday' as they began their march north. An alternative version of the story claims that 'Black Friday' was the name used by alarmed Londoners when they discovered that the Jacobite army was as close as Derby. The novelist Henry Fielding wrote, "When the Highlanders by a most incredible march got between the army of the Duke of Cumberland and the metropolis they struck a terror into it scarce to be credited". There was a run on the Bank of England, which paid out in sixpenny pieces to gain time.

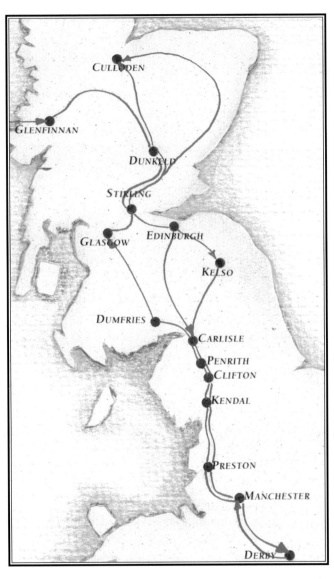

CULLODEN

GLENFINNAN

DUNKELD

STIRLING

GLASGOW   EDINBURGH

KELSO

DUMFRIES

CARLISLE

PENRITH
CLIFTON

KENDAL

PRESTON

MANCHESTER

DERBY

A map showing the progress of the Jacobites to Derby and their retreat back to the Highlands.

The Prince's troops took the same route northwards as they had on the hopeful descent towards the capital, only this time the mood was far from euphoric, with Charles sulking for most of the journey.

Wade and Cumberland pursued the retreating Jacobite army, though the winter weather made travel difficult for everyone concerned. On 18th December Lord George Murray masterminded a victorious Jacobite skirmish which checked Cumberland and his men at Clifton Moor near Penrith, close to the modern A6 road in what is now the county of Cumbria.

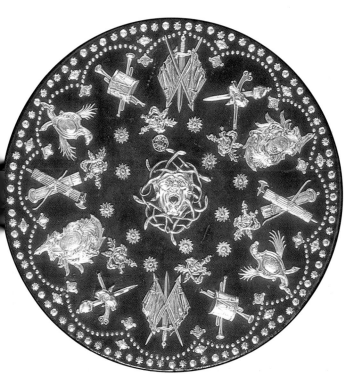

Bonnie Prince Charlie's targe.

This encounter was significant as the last battle to be fought on English soil, and also for its influence on the undoubtedly brutal treatment meted out to Jacobite soldiers in the aftermath of the Battle of Culloden the following April.

Cumberland noted in his official report of Clifton Moor that when some of his officers fell injured, Jacobite soldiers shouted "No quarter! Murder them!", and they received several wounds after they were knocked down'. The Jacobite troops had also been reputedly less than fastidious in their treatment of government wounded in the aftermath of Prestonpans.

On 20th December Charles and his men crossed the River Esk at Longtown back into Scotland, leaving their garrison at Carlisle to surrender to Cumberland after a brief siege. Stirling town surrendered to the Jacobites, though its castle held out as Edinburgh had done, and fresh Scottish recruits and some newly-arrived French troops boosted the Jacobite force to around eight thousand.

One of the most famous of all Scottish songs is the ballad The Banks of Loch Lomond, *which was reputedly written by a Jacobite prisoner awaiting execution in Carlisle jail. The lines "For ye'll tak the high road and I'll tak the low road, and I'll be in Scotland afore ye" are thought to refer to the fact that the writer's soul would return to his homeland before his living compatriots.*

Lieutenant-General Henry Hawley — ominously known to his men as 'Hangman Hawley' because of his fondness for erecting and using gibbets — had succeeded Cumberland as commander by this time, with Cumberland having been recalled to face the threat of a French invasion force on the south coast of England.

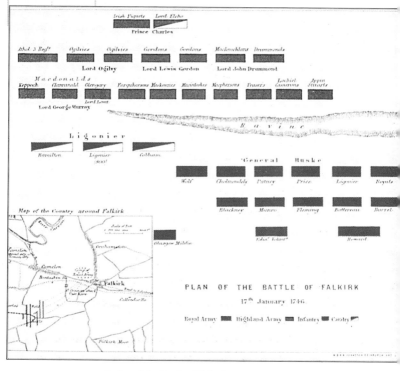

A plan of the Battle of Falkirk.

Hawley and his troops marched from Edinburgh to relieve the government garrison at Stirling, and on 17th January they were soundly defeated by a numerically inferior force of Jacobites to the south-west of Falkirk. Unfortunately, Charles and his men failed to capitalise on their victory and allowed Hawley time to regroup his forces.

It is said that townsfolk watched the battle from an earlier version of Falkirk's best-known landmark, the Steeple, which gives an idea of just how close the battlefield was to the town. A monument near Greenbank now marks the site, just south of the Union Canal which was constructed in 1820.

Stirling Castle. There has been a stronghold on this dramatic site since the eleventh century.

Whilst besieging Stirling Castle the Prince stayed at Bannockburn House, owned by Sir Hugh Paterson, and among the party entertaining Charles was his host's niece, Clementina Walkinshaw, who was to become his mistress and later bear him the illegitimate daughter Charlotte, who was to be a source of comfort in his final years.

Though Charles resided at Bannockburn, there was to be no repeat of Robert The Bruce's famous victory over the English forces of Edward II, which gave Scotland her freedom from England in 1314.

Falkirk 29th January 1746

We think it our duty in this critical
Juncture to lay our opinions in the most respectful manner
before your Royal Highness. —

We are certain that a vast number of the soldiers
of your Royal Highness's Army are gone home since the
Battle of Falkirk; and notwithstanding all the endeavours
of the Commanders of the different Corps, they find that this
evil is increasing hourly, and not in their power to prevent
and as we are afraid Sterling Castle cannot be taken so
soon as was expected, if the enemy should march before it
fall into your R.H's hands, we can forsee nothing but utter
distruction to the few that will remain, considering the in-
equality of our numbers to that of the Enemy. — For these
Reasons we are humbly of opinion that there is no way left
to extricate your R.H. and those who remain with you, out
of the most imminent danger, but by retiring immediately to the
Highlands where we can be usefully employed the remainder
of the Winter by taking and mastering the Forts in the North,
and we are morally sure we can keep as many men together
as will answer that end, hinder the enemy from following us
in the mountains at this season of the year; And in spring
we doubt not but an Army of Ten thousand effective Highlanders
can be brought together and follow your R.H. wherever
you think proper; this will certainly disconcert your ene-
mies and cannot but be approved of by your R.H's friends
both at home and abroad, if a landing should happen in the
mean time, the Highlanders would immediately rise either
to Join them, or to make a powerful diversion elsewhere. —

The hard Marches which your Army have
undergone

The Retreat Continues

In the aftermath of the Battle of Falkirk, Cumberland returned to take over command from Hawley. With the government forces again ready to march, a shortage of supplies and the prospect of serious Jacobite desertions, Murray and the chiefs insisted that the only sensible course of action was to retreat to the Highlands for the remainder of the winter, before launching a spring offensive, when it was thought ten thousand men could be put into the field.

Not surprisingly, Charles did not agree, arguing that such a course of action would once and for all remove any possibility of a large-scale French assault in support of the Jacobites and deter the supply of any other foreign assistance.

He recorded his objections to the proposed retreat in a letter to the clan chiefs, in which he disclaimed all personal responsibility for such a plan, and on 1st February 1746 the Jacobite forces crossed the Forth and headed north, followed inexorably by Cumberland's army.

The Jacobites reached Inverness on 18th February, taking the castle two days later. For seven weeks Charles was based in a house in Church Street in the Highland capital.

THE BATTLE OF CULLODEN

By the 15th April Cumberland was at Nairn, some sixteen miles to the east, where he celebrated his twenty-fifth birthday in camp with his troops, while Charles and the Jacobite army assembled at Drumossie Moor, now known as Culloden, five miles east of Inverness, ready to do battle with the government forces. The night before the battle, Charles stayed at Culloden House, home of Duncan Forbes, Lord President of the Court of Session, and now the Culloden House Hotel.

Culloden House as it is today.

William Augustus, Duke of Cumberland, (1721–1765).

William Augustus, Duke of Cumberland, third son of George II, was four months younger than Prince Charles, to whom he presented a great contrast, both physically and emotionally. Already a bulky, ponderous figure, Cumberland was a cool professional soldier who possessed the invaluable ability to inspire total confidence in his men, without being a military genius. Despite his youth, he was a shrewd and highly experienced commander, who had led a 50,000-strong allied army at the Battle of Fontenoy in May 1745 during the War of the Austrian Succession.

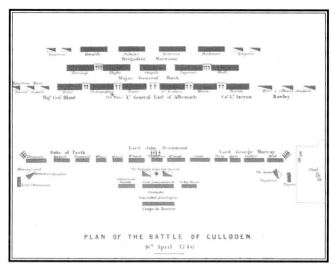

A plan of the Battle of Culloden.

The Jacobite situation was hindered by the serious differences that existed between its leaders. Lord George Murray, the pragmatic professional soldier, was by now very much at odds with his Prince, who still retained an unreal optimism about events that were becoming more desperate by the day.

Had Murray been allowed to choose the place where the Jacobite army was to make its stand, then the outcome of the subsequent battle might have been considerably different. Unfortunately for the Highlanders, however, the Prince had taken personal command, and accepted the far from sound advice of his Irish Adjutant-General John O'Sullivan on where to fight.

Murray was later to write, "There could never be a more improper ground for Highlanders", and in a letter to the Prince after Culloden he made the remark, worthy of Oscar Wilde, that "I wish Mr O'Sullivan had never got any other charge in the Army than the care of the bagage (sic) which I have been told he was brought up to understand" !

The battlefield of Culloden is now in the care of the National Trust for Scotland, and includes a Memorial Cairn (1801), the Graves of the Clans, and the Well of the Dead — where the body of Alexander MacGillivray was found. MacGillivray led the men of Clan Chattan whose charge was strong enough to break through Cumberland's first line of defence, before their leader was killed. Other features include The Keppoch Stone, which marks the spot where Alistair MacDonnell of Keppoch fell, The English Stone, where the English dead were reputedly buried, and the Cumberland Stone — where the Duke is supposed to have eaten a hasty meal after the battle, and perhaps studied the lie of the land before it. Old Leanach Cottage is furnished in period style, and there is also a modern visitor centre. Realignment of the road which previously bisected the batttlefield and the felling of conifer trees has restored the field of Culloden to something close to its state in 1746.

The open, boggy moorland of Drumossie was totally unsuitable for the Highlanders' principal method of attack, the charge, and greatly favoured Cumberland's artillery and cavalry. With regard to the entire episode of Culloden, Charles showed a sad lack of military understanding, and persisted in believing that a charge by his troops in any circumstances would be sure to win him another battle.

Correctly anticipating disaster if the Jacobite army fought on Drumossie Moor, Lord George Murray suggested a night attack on Cumberland's camp at Nairn, where the men were celebrating their commander's birthday with brandy.

This plan proved abortive, however, as day was dawning with the Jacobites still two miles from Cumberland's camp, and a retreat to Drumossie meant that by the time battle was joined, Charles' men were tired both by the march and by lack of sleep. They were also suffering from a shortage of food.

A contemporary engraving of the Battle of Culloden.

With a strength of nine thousand, Cumberland's army was nearly twice the size of the Prince's, and shortly after 11am on 16th April the Duke's artillery opened up on the Jacobite forces to devastating effect. The only realistic answer at this point was for the Highlanders to charge, exactly as Cumberland had anticipated. Those Jacobites who survived the firepower of the government troops were caught by bayonets, and in little more than half an hour the last pitched battle to be fought on British soil was over, and the final Stuart rising was at an end.

After the battle, more than one thousand of the Jacobite forces lay dead, and Charles was led, bewildered, from the field as his surviving troops withdrew. According to some accounts, he left in tears.

There are many necessarily apocryphal stories of individual acts of heroism at Culloden, including one concerning Gillies MacBean of Clan Chattan, who reputedly killed thirteen redcoats single-handedly, despite suffering severe wounds, before being trampled by dragoons' horses and fatally injured. Cameron of Lochiel was wounded in both legs during the battle.

A contemporary engraving of the Battle of Culloden.

A highly unorthodox use of whisky occurred at Culloden, as related by Bishop Forbes in his Journal... "Mr John Maitland... administered the Holy Eucharist to Lord Strathallan on the Culloden field, it is said, with oat-cake and whisky, the requisite elements not being attainable".

> *The lovely lass of Inverness*
> *Nae joy nor pleasure can she see;*
> *For e'en and morn she cries, alas!*
> *And aye the saut tear blin's her ee:*
> *Drumossie Moor – Drumossie day –*
> *A waefu' day it was to me !*
> *For there I lost my father dear,*
> *My father dear, and brethren three.*

from Lament For Culloden, *by Robert Burns*

THE AFTERMATH OF DEFEAT

Despite the romantic legends that have grown up to cloak the final days of the '45, it has to be said that Charles' conduct both at, and in the aftermath of, Culloden left much to be desired in its apparent disregard for the men who had followed him from the start of his doubtful enterprise.

Prior to the battle, Charles had made no provision for a rendezvous site should things go badly for his forces, and when the bulk of the Jacobite survivors assembled at Ruthven under Lord George Murray, they received a message from their Prince which read "Let every man seek his safety the best way he can". There was no expression of gratitude for the sacrifices made, and he also took most of what funds remained in the Jacobite coffers to facilitate his own escape.

After Culloden, Lord George Murray never saw Charles again. He hid in Glenartney for eight months, before escaping to the continent, where he travelled extensively, living in Germany and dying at Medemblik in Holland in 1760.

The five months between Charles' defeat at Culloden and his eventual evacuation to France were distinguished by many individual acts of courage and heroism. Had it not been for a residual regard and respect for the fugitive Prince himself, as much as for the cause he espoused, the generous reward which was placed on his head by the government would surely have been claimed. As Lady Nairne's song Will Ye No Come Back Again? puts it, "English bribes were a' in vain/An' e'en tho' puirer we may be;/Siller canna buy the heart/That beats aye for thine and thee".

48

A contemporary engraving of the execution of Lord Lovat.

Whilst Charles was in hiding, the people of the Highlands were paying a terrible price for their support of the Stuart cause. Cumberland's troops acted with indefensible brutality both on the battlefield of Culloden, where they slaughtered many Jacobite wounded, and subsequently in the devastation they wreaked on Jacobite and non-Jacobite Highlanders, men, women and children, "He created a desert and called it peace", is one evocative description of Cumberland's treatment of the Highlands, taken from Tacitus' quotation of Calgacus (A.D. 84).

One of Cumberland's own officers wrote that the Duke's men on the field of Culloden "Looked like so many butchers rather than Christian soldiers". The sobriquet 'butcher' was soon applied to Cumberland himself by the Highlanders, though back in London he was afforded a hero's welcome. Handel composed The Conquering Hero for his triumphal return, and the flower Sweet William was named in his honour. In Scotland a weed was called Stinking Willie in retaliation.

One hundred and twenty Jacobite prisoners were executed following Culloden, including four peers who were accorded the privilege of beheading rather than the more lingering practice of hanging, drawing and quartering meted out to the commoners. Simon Fraser, Lord Lovat, became the last peer to die by the axe, on 9th April 1747. Nearly a thousand Jacobites were transported to the colonies, and a further two hundred were allowed to choose their own countries of exile.

THE PRINCE ON THE RUN

The story of Charles' life as a fugitive during the 157 days spent on the run after Culloden could fill a book in itself, and has, in fact, filled several. Whatever his shortcomings, it is apparent that whilst in hiding the Prince showed the courage and fortitude that had so endeared him to the clansmen during the earlier stages of the campaign. The MacDonald chief Lochgarry wrote "Show me a King or Prince in Europe cou'd have borne the like, or the tenth part of it". Charles suffered the depredations of lice, dysentery, hunger, and that menace of the West Highlands that the passing of two centuries has done nothing to diminish, the midge.

In the immediate aftermath of Culloden, Charles spent time hiding out by Loch Arkaig, close to the spot where the standard had been raised at Glenfinnan, and his fugitive wanderings took him from Loch nan Uamh, where he had originally landed, to the Hebridean island of Benbecula on 27th April.

Close to Loch Arkaig at the heart of Clan Cameron country stands a long avenue of beech trees which once formed a canopy over the road, giving rise to the name, 'The Dark Mile'. This was one of Charles' hiding places after Culloden. At the end of the Dark Mile, on the shores of the loch, the elusive 'Arkaig Treasure' is reputedly buried. This was a large sum of money and a supply of arms, delivered into Loch Arkaig by the French, who were unaware that the Battle of Culloden had been fought and the Prince's cause lost.

From Benbecula Charles moved to Lewis and South Uist, then crossed to the Isle of Skye, before being shipped back to the mainland once again, all the while pursued by government troops, who searched the islands and had ships stationed in the Minch. At times the soldiers were very close, and it was their proximity that necessitated Charles' swift evacuation from Uist to Skye towards the end of June.

The Prince's cairn at Loch nan Uamh marks the place where Charles departed for France in September 1746.

FLORA MACDONALD

At this point the figure of Flora MacDonald, the most famous female Jacobite, enters the story. Of all the heroes and heroines who aided the Prince, Flora stands supreme. She became the ultimate romantic symbol of all that was purest and most notable about the Cause, a pretty, unsophisticated young woman only too anxious to be of service to her handsome Prince. "A very pritty young rebel", as a government officer described her in a letter of 1746.

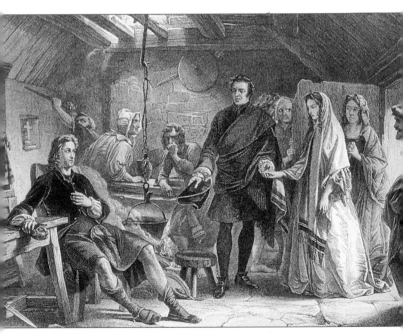

A Victorian depiction of the first meeting between Flora MacDonald and Bonnie Prince Charlie.

In reality, Flora was the step-daughter of a government militia captain and had recently returned to Skye from a formal education in Edinburgh. When approached, she was also initially more worried than thrilled at the prospect of playing a leading role in the Jacobite drama.

Flora had been born in 1722 on the island of South Uist, and she facilitated the Prince's escape by dressing him as her supposed maid, an Irishwoman by the name of Betty Burke. Flora's apprehension had been reasonable, as the sea crossing on 28th June was rough, and once landed on Skye, she had to escort her 'maid' across the island to Portree, running the gauntlet of militiamen along the way.

On parting in Portree, Charles is reputed to have given Flora a lock of his hair and said "For all that has happened, Madam, I hope we shall meet in St James' yet". In fact they were never to meet again, and Charles was never to see St James'. The lock of hair survives, however, like so many more given by the Prince as keepsakes, and is on display in Dunvegan Castle, the Skye home of Clan MacLeod — supporters of King George II.

On the Isle of Skye, Flora MacDonald's grave and monument is located at Kilmuir, on the Trotternish peninsula, while in Portree the room where the Prince and Flora said their farewells is now part of the Royal Hotel. There are plans to construct a bronze depicting their last meeting overlooking Portree Harbour. The whisky-based liqueur Drambuie is reputedly made to a recipe given by Prince Charles to the Mackinnon family of Skye in return for their

assistance during his time on the island, and was first concocted at
the Broadford Hotel.

On her return to Uist, Flora was arrested and imprisoned for a year for her part in Charles' escape. In 1750 she married her kinsman Alan MacDonald and the couple emigrated to America, where Flora was met with acclaim for her role in the Jacobite rising. She finally returned to Skye, where she died in March 1790.

Dr Samuel Johnson met Flora when he visited the Hebrides with James Boswell in 1773, and described her as a woman of "...middle stature, soft features, gentle manners, and elegant presence. Her name will be mentioned in history, and if courage and fidelity are virtues, mentioned with honour".

Speed bonnie boat like a bird on the wing,
Onward the sailors cry;
Carry the lad that is born to be king,
Over the sea to Skye.

Though the waves leap, soft shall ye sleep,
Ocean's a royal bed:
Rocked in the deep, Flora will keep
Watch by your weary head.

The Skye Boat Song

RETURN TO EXILE

From Skye, Charles was taken to the mainland at Mallaig, and back into the wilds of the West Highlands, where he was still in great danger and continued to live rough for much of the time. Then, on 19th September he boarded the French ship L'Heureux at Loch nan Uamh, and fourteen months after his arrival at the same place, he sailed for France. He was accompanied by the faithful Cameron of Lochiel and more than one hundred other followers, and arrived in France twenty days later. Lochiel, along with Lochgarry and Clanranald, obtained a commission in the French army. A memorial cairn now stands on the shores of Loch nan Uamh to mark the place of departure (see page 51).

Charles was physically safe, but the story of the rest of his life is one of sad anti-climax and disappointment, the 'Bonnie Prince' becoming a figure who was far from 'bonnie' in later years. Effectively, the most meaningful part of his life had been lived during those astonishing fourteen months of 1745–6, and portraits of Charles in exile show a bloated and unhealthy man, with eyes that hold a terrible sadness.

On arrival in France, Charles was greeted with great popular enthusiasm, but Louis XV offered him a pension rather than the twenty thousand troops he requested for another attempt on the British throne. Charles' refusal to accept defeat — or the pension — finally exasperated Louis, who eventually had him deported. Charles still believed that a Stuart revival was possible, and in 1750, and it is believed in 1753, he visited London incognito, but nothing came of his plans and dreams.

THE FINAL YEARS

Drink had always been one of Charles' potential weaknesses, and in frustrated exile its potential was sadly fulfilled. In 1753 he and his mistress Clementina Walkinshaw had a daughter, Charlotte, but seven years later Clementina left him, taking Charlotte with her.

In 1765 he visited his dying father, whom he had previously been unable to face, in Rome, but the 'Old Pretender' was already dead by the time his son arrived. The Pope allowed Charles to live as a member of Roman society, but his role in that society was to receive a setback when his subsequent marriage to the young German Princess Louise of Stolberg — thirty years his junior — effectively ended as a result of a particularly gruelling St Andrew's Day spree in 1780.

Formal separation followed four years later, after which Charles was reconciled with his daughter, legitimising her as the Duchess of Albany. Charlotte was to be a great source of comfort to her father in his last years. She nursed him through mental and physical illness in Florence until his death by a paralytic stroke on 31st January 1788.

Charles died without legitimate issue, and his brother Henry, Duke of York, who had become a cardinal in 1747, gave him a royal funeral. He was buried initially at Frascati near Rome, and was later reinterred in the crypt of St Peter's in Rome alongside his father and brother. Henry died in 1807, the last of the direct Stuart line.

In 1819 the sculptor Antonio Canova was commissioned by Pope Pius VII to create a memorial, and the Prince Regent, later George IV, gave £50 towards its cost. George III had previously granted Henry a pension to support him in his later years, after the French had invaded Italy and taken possession of his estates. To the Jacobite faithful, Henry was King Henry I and IX, just as Charles had been King Charles III.

CHANGES IN THE HIGHLANDS

While Charles was living out the greater part of his life in exile, the Highlands of Scotland and its people were undergoing radical and far-reaching changes.

It would be wrong to think of the Highlands as we see them today — with their empty glens and legacy of exile and depopulation to marginal coastal areas — as a direct result of the final Jacobite rebellion. The events of 1745–6 did not lead immediately to the Highland Clearances as is often supposed; rather they led to the alteration of the social structure of the Highlands in such a way that the clearances became possible, as they would not have been with the prevailing paternalistic clan system that existed before the events of 1745–6.

After Culloden, the government introduced a number of measures which were quite blatantly calculated to destroy the clan-based system and to remove by legislation anything which made the Highlands a place apart from the rest of Britain. In this way it was supposed that any future Jacobite attempts would fail to take root in their natural heartland where the chiefs' word had previously been law.

Highland dress was declared illegal, weapons had to be surrendered, estates were forfeited, and most significantly of all, the essential power of the clan chiefs was removed, leaving them as very little more than glorified landlords. Taking no chances, the government strengthened Fort William and rebuilt Fort Augustus, and at Inverness a new Fort George was constructed, eleven miles north-east of the town.

THE LEGEND

What the ill-fated Jacobite rising of 1745–6 gave to Scotland in positive terms was its greatest legend, which soon began to be celebrated in story, poem and song. Success would surely not have created such a lasting body of literature and music.

Robert Burns and James Hogg both wrote Jacobite material, with Hogg editing The Jacobite Relics of Scotland, published in 1819–21, to which he contributed the popular song Charlie is My Darling and the less well known Donald MacGillivray. Carolina Oliphant, Lady Nairne, contributed a number of ballads to the canon of Jacobite music, most notably Will Ye No' Come Back Again?

Queen Victoria was a professed Jacobite sympathiser and admirer of the Highlands, and during her reign much writing celebrated the '45 rising and the Highland character in general. At the forefront of this Celtic renaissance was Sir Walter Scott, whose first — and anonymously published — novel Waverley (1814) takes the '45 as its subject matter.

The character of Fergus Mac Ivor from Sir Walter Scott's Jacobite novel, Waverley.

It is perhaps worth musing here on what might have happened had Charles succeeded in recapturing the British throne for the Stuarts in 1745–6.

Inevitably, he would have gone down in history as just another monarch, probably one who fought his erstwhile allies the French and lost the American colonies. Perhaps his greatest good fortune was to have failed, to be remembered by history like a rock star who died young, a Jimi Hendrix or a Jim Morrison of Jacobitism.

And legend has served Bonnie Prince Charlie well, even though he did not die young. Few now think of him as an embittered, alcoholic wife-beater, bloated with drink, legs ulcerated, surrounded by debts and regrets for what might have been. Instead, the romantic legend of a million shortbread tins lives on.

It is best, perhaps, to think of the Charles Edward Stuart who drank rough whisky with his clansmen and earned their respect for his courage and physical stamina, wearing dirty clothes, with several days' growth of stubble, hiding out after Culloden in 'Cluny's Cage' on the slopes of Ben Alder, his spirit not yet broken. Truly then he could have been a king.

Bonnie Charlie's now awa,

Safely owre the friendly main;

Mony a heart will break in twa,

Should he ne'er come back again.

Will ye no come back again?

Will ye no come back again?

Better lo'ed ye canna be,

Will ye no come back again?

Will Ye No' Come Back Again?
Carolina Oliphant, Lady Nairne

Selected Places of Interest to Visit

Holyrood Palace and Edinburgh Castle, City of Edinburgh, Edinburgh Tourist Board: 0131 557 1700.

Pass of Killiecrankie, 3 miles north of Pitlochry, Perthshire, just off the A9, National Trust for Scotland. Blair Castle, 7 miles north of Pitlochry, Perthshire, also close to the A9, in the village of Blair Atholl. Perth Tourist Information Office: 01738 627959.

Ruthven Barracks, close to the A9 near Kingussie, 45 miles south of Inverness, Historic Scotland. Fort George, 11 miles north-east of Inverness, on B9006, off the A96 Inverness-Aberdeen road, Historic Scotland. Culloden Battlefield and Visitor Centre, 5 miles east of Inverness on the B9006, National Trust for Scotland. Inverness Tourist Information Office: 01463 234353.

West Highland Museum, Cameron Square, Fort William, Inverness-shire. The Glenfinnan Monument and Visitor Centre, 14 miles west of Fort William on the A830 Fort William–Mallaig road, National Trust for Scotland. Fort William Tourist Information Office: 01397 703781.

Isle of Skye Tourist Information Centre (Portree): 01478 612137. Outer Hebrides Tourist Board (Stornoway, Isle of Lewis): 01851 3088. National Trust for Scotland, 5 Charlotte Square, Edinburgh EH2 4DU: 0131 226 5922. Historic Scotland, 20 Brandon Street, Edinburgh EH3 5RA: 0131 244 3101.

INDEX

America 54, 60
Anne, Queen 10, 12
Arisaig 20

Bank of England 33
Bannockburn House 38
battles 5
  Culloden 12, 22, 36, 41–7, 48, 49, 58, 60
  Falkirk 16, 37–9, 40
  Killiecrankie 8, 9, 25
  Prestonpans 16, 26–8, 29, 36
  Sherrifmuir 11
Benbecula 50, 51
Black Friday 33
Black Watch 14
Blair Castle 25, 62
Bonnie Dundee 8
Boswell, James 54
Burns, Robert 47, 59

cairns 5, 27, 44, 51, 55
Cameron, Donald 23, 46, 55
Canova, Antonio 56
Carlisle 30, 36
Catholic faith 7, 8, 11, 17, 29, 56, 57
Chain, the 13
clans
  Cameron 23, 50
  Chattan 44, 46
  Fraser 28, 49
  MacDonald 28
  MacDonalds of Glencoe 23, 62
  MacDonalds of Keppoch 23, 24, 44
  MacLeod 53
  Macpherson 28
  Stewarts of Appin 28
Clifton Moor 35, 36
Cope, General Sir John 24
Cumberland, William Augustus, Duke of 32,
  35, 36, 40, 41, 42, 44, 45, 46, 49
Cumbria 6, 35
Culloden House 41

Dark Mile, the 50
Derby 31, 32–6
Douglas, Clementina Johannes Sobieski 6
Drummond, James Duke of Perth 24, 25
Drummond John 32
Drumossie Moor — see Battle of Culloden
Du Teillay 19, 20
Dunbar 27

Edinburgh 24, 25, 27, 28, 29, 36, 37, 53, 62
Elcho, Lord 33
Elizabeth, The 19
Eriskay, island of 19, 20

Fielding, Henry 33
Finchley Common 32, 33
food 28, 45
Fort Augustus 13, 14, 58
Fort George 14, 58, 62
Fort William 13, 14, 22, 23, 58, 62
France 11, 18, 19, 24, 29, 32, 26, 40, 48, 50, 55, 60

Gaelic, 21, 22
George I, King 11
George II, King 21, 29, 32, 42
George IV, King 57
Glenfinnan 21, 22, 24, 50, 62
Glorious Revolution 7, 8

Hanoverian weather 11, 18
Hawley, Lieutenant-General Henry 36, 37, 40
Hebrides 19, 50, 51, 62
Henry, Duke of York 17, 56, 57
Highland Clearances 58
Historic Scotland 13, 62
Hogg, James 59
Holyrood Palace 28, 62

Inverness 13, 15, 40, 41, 58
Irish 7, 20, 43, 44
Italy 16, 17, 56, 57

James VII and II, 7, 8, 10, 11
Johnson, Dr Samuel 54

Kendal 3
Killiecrankie, Pass of 9, 62

Lancaster 29
Lewis 51
L'Heureux 55
Lochgarry 50, 55
Loch Arkaig 50
Loch nan Uamh 20, 50, 51, 55
Loch Sheil 21
London 25, 27, 29, 31, 33, 55
Lovat, Lord 28, 49
Louis XV, King 55
Louise of Stolberg 56
Lowlands 7, 14, 24, 29

MacBean, Gillies 46
MacDonald, Flora 52–4

MacDonnell, Alistair 44
MacGillivray, Alexander 44, 59
Manchester 30, 31
Manchester Regiment 31
Mar, Earl of 11
Mary, Queen 8
Murray, Lord George, 24, 25, 31, 32, 35, 40, 43, 44, 45, 48
museums 5, 23, 62

Nairn 41, 45
National Trust for Scotland 9, 22, 44, 62

Old Pretender 11, 16, 21, 56
Oliphant, Carolina (Lady Nairne) 48, 59, 61
O'Sullivan, John 20, 43, 44

Paterson, Sir Hugh 38
Perth 6, 24, 28, 62
Perth, Duke of 24, 25
Pope Clement XI 17
Pope Pius VII 56, 57
Portree 53
Preston 30

roads 13–15
Robert the Bruce 38
Ruthven Barracks 13, 14, 48, 62

Scott, Sir Walter 59
Seven Men of Moidart 20
Sobieski, Clementina 16
South Uist 51, 53
Spain 11, 18
Stirling 15, 36, 37, 38
Stuart, Charlotte 38, 56

toast (drinking) 10, 23
Tullibardine

Marquis of 21, 24
Victoria, Queen 59
visitor centres 5, 6, 22, 62

Wade, Major-General George 13–15, 32, 35
Walkinshaw, Clementina 6, 38, 56
Waverley 59
Welsh 7
West Highland Museum, Fort William 23, 62
whisky 47, 53, 60
William of Orange 8, 10

Photographic Acknowledgements

Aberdeen University Library, William Macbean Collection: Cover (top) and pages 10, 12, 14, 15, 18, 26, 26-7, 30-31, 32–3, 37, 43, 45, 47, 49, 52, 59. Edinburgh Photographic Library: Cover (main) and pages 9, 13, 22, 25, 28, 38, 41, 44, 51. Editor's pictures: 7, 8, 29. Mansell Collection: Page 42. Scottish National Gallery: Page 5. Scottish National Museums and Galleries: Title page and page 35. Scottish National Record Office: Page 39. West Highland Museum: Pages 16, 17, 23, 60.